Chess Jokes

The Biggest Book Ever! Over 300 Original Puns

Danny Trevanion

Any similarity to these jokes to existing jokes in other books, movies, games or published anywhere else is purely coincidental. This book is not affiliated with any chess organisation or company. this is designed simply as a fun book for chess fans.

All rights reserved. No part of this publication may be reproduced, distributed, or transmitted in any form or by any means, including photocopying, recording, or other electronic or mechanical methods, without the prior written permission of the publisher, except in the case of brief quotations embodied in critical reviews and certain other noncommercial uses permitted by copyright law.

Danny Trevanion has asserted the right to be the author of this work.

Copyright 2023

Contents

You Must Be Joking, Danny!	1
Introduction	2
Opening Gambit Jokes	5
Grandmaster Jokes	29
Middlegame Jokes	37
Endgame Jokes	57
Checkmate!	82
Notes	83

You Must Be Joking, Danny!

All these jokes are original. Some are good, some are bad, some are all out weird. Some will make you laugh; some will make you smile; some will make you think, some will make you roll your eyes.

Many of these jokes a lot of people will get, but some are just for the *superfans*.

All are to be celebrated.

Remember:

We learn the more we see in different ways.

When we embrace the silliness, we have a better time and enjoy the ride more.

Introduction

I've been interested in chess since I was introduced to it by my father when I was around five. I would play at school whenever I could and probably would have joined a chess club if I had known they existed. When I wasn't playing with family members or friends, I would play on my PC against Chessmaster, Battle Chess, Waxman, or programs I had long forgotten. One Christmas, I received a Kasparov Chess Challenger, a computer with a chessboard, which I still have and occasionally play with. However, I was a relative newcomer to the world of chess apps about six years ago, mainly because they had websites I didn't use much prior. I had fun exploring Chess 24, Chess.com and Li Chess, and the more novel apps that have come along the way. I got addicted to the adrenaline and dopamine hits that bullet chess provided me so much that I had to abstain for several months and be careful even now.

Although I'm not very good at chess, I will be, at best, a middling player now that I am approaching a middling age. I am perpetually interested in playing and have watched the coverage of many major tournaments on YouTube and Chess 24, which I thoroughly enjoy.

I felt it, therefore, natural to combine my love of jokes with my passion for chess, which I compiled over many months. Sometimes I would think of them when playing, especially while waiting my turn or watching the Chess Champions Tour during 2022.

I have done my best to group sets of jokes so you are more likely to understand and appreciate their form of them. The disadvantage is it may seem like beating a dead horse if you're not enjoying that particular type of gag! As always in this Jokes for Superfans series, I don't expect readers to understand every pun. Many are created when by colliding two worlds together. Even if you get the chess reference (and some of these are pretty obscure), you may not understand the other one. I was born, educated and live in England, so my bias is towards that location. The phraseology and references certainly reflect this. These jokes are also created for all age groups. Although children won't understand many of the jokes, if you are a young person, I hope you keep coming back to this book, and it is something you can grow up with. I didn't fully understand many of my favourite books from childhood, but that made them a source of great learning. Many of these jokes will also be appreciated at different ages and various life stages. So please don't feel bad or frustrated or end up down some rabbit hole searching for what I may mean. If you like, you can always contact me @dannytrevanion on social media, and I'll do my best to explain the splurges from my brain.

The strange quality of jokes is they are incredibly subjective. Even jokes I've created and don't believe are funny, I tell them to somebody, and they laugh – or at least think it's clever or interesting – and I'll even take that. This is why I tell my readers if they don't like a joke, move on to the next one; they may enjoy that one better. With over 300 in this particular collection, it would be remarkable if you understood them all, let alone raise a smile on your face. Many 'will likely raise your eyebrows. That's always the risk in creating such a niche list of jokes. However, I recommend going through this collection and finding your favourites so you can break some tension or inject some laughs during your next chess game, whether in person or online.

I have grouped these gags together, much like a chess game, however many jokes can be "played" however you like. Hopefully you will employ your own mental strength and stategies in getting to the end without getting mated. I sincerely hope you enjoy this fun compilation of my original jokes about the wonderful game of chess.

Danny Trevanion, January 2023

Opening Gambit Jokes

♛

What other chess piece can jump like a knight?

A BisHOP

♛

Why do you never see a grandmaster smile?

When their photo is taken they say "chess".

How does a OCD chess player play his endgame?

   Neat as a pin

Who was the greatest player in the wild west?

   Chessie James

What do you call an old grandmaster?

   Magnus Carlsenior

How do chickens play chess?

   With a chess cluck

How is attacking by doubling up pieces like an electromagnetic induction?

    Both are charging batteries

What do chess players say before bed?

    Knighty Knight

Why do grandmasters admire conker players?

    Because they're chess nuts

How does a knitter play chess?

    Under and over the board

♛

How does a player go up in ranking?

   On a chesseculator

♛

What is a grandmaster's favourite drink?

   A chesspresso

♛

How does a grandmaster calculate odds?

   Using his best chesstimation

♛

Why is playing good for depression?

   Because it increases a player's self-chessteam

What do you call two grandmasters who get divorced?

   Chesstranged

A child prodigy beating a grandmaster – the best way to chesstablish onto the scene.

What the best way to develop a team of grandmasters?

   Chessprit De Corps

What do you call a cold grandmaster?

   A chesskimo

♛

Note for commentators: Rare happenings in the game should be dubbed "chesspecial".

♛

What publication is exclusively for male players?

Chessquire Magazine

♛

How are tournament winners paid in Portugal?

In chesscudos

♛

The most successful player can build amass the largest fortunes and the biggest chesstates.

There was once a mythical tale of a grandmaster's game, which he first heard as a song from a dream whilst waking up. It's known as Chessterday

I couldn't find another name for a grandmaster so I checked the Chessaurus.

The oldest player is so old he nicknamed 'chessaurus'.

What is a grandmasters favourite food?

    Chesscalopes

A referee thought he saw a player cheating with his phone but didn't wish to chessculate the issue.

♛

Harry Houdini's rating was so high he was known as the Amazing Chesscapologist.

♛

What is a grandmaster's favourite shoe?

Chesspradrilles

♛

How does a player think abstractly?

By refining their chessoteric knowledge.

♛

To become a great player you first have to learn the basic chessentials.

The player able to manoeuvre out of a fatal mistake can be referred to a chesscapee.

What do you call a chess player who is briefly sighted performing hip hop?

    Grandmaster Flash

What do you call a Russian grandmaster at a 45 degree angle?

    Boris Spassky Slopes

What do you get if you cross a dog with a grandmaster?

    Gary Kasparover

♛

What do you call a grandmaster who cheats?

   Peter Swindler

♛

When you're an a losing streak it's just best to get Karpover it.

♛

Who are fastest chess players?

   The Rush-sians

♛

What do you get if you cross a grandmaster with a toaster?

   Paul Morphy Richards

♛

What do you call an infinitely recurring grandmaster?

CHESS JOKES

Vishy Anandandandandand

♛

What do you call a grandmaster behind his back?

Wesley So and So

♛

How do you pose a question to a female player?

Get Emanuel 'L'asker

♛

How does a grandmaster gain a sense of perspective.

Ask KarP.O.V.

♛

What do you call a grandmaster who is always making mistakes?

Levan Erronian

♛

What happens if a chess player dies?

   Inform his next Karjakin

♛

What do you call the most refined and cultured grandmaster?

   Ding Lirenaissance Man

♛

What do you call a overworked grandmaster?

   Hikaru Knackermura

♛

What do you call a grandmaster from another dimension?

   Richard Rapported

Which grandmaster has the softest touch?

   Paul Caress

Which grandmaster often got out of shape when he lost?

   Bent Larsen

Humphrey Bogart starring in *Capablanca* would have been a very different movie:
  "We'll always have Paris gambit"

What do you call a chess player who eats all his greens?

   Alexander Alkaline

♛

Knock knock.
　Who's there?
　Guess.
　Guess Who?
　No, wrong board game – chess's Dominguez

♛

What do you call a grandmaster who steals?

　A Larsen-ist

♛

What service unties chess players locally?

　Yik Yakovich

♛

　Knock knock
　Who's there?
　Yifan.

CHESS JOKES

Yifan who?
No. Hou Yifan!

♛

Sometimes it seems Anish is mechanical the way he ups his tempo and switches Giri like that.

♛

What do you call a chess player who doesn't practice?

   Can't be Radjabovvered

♛

What do you call a grandmaster who protects their tent?
Judit Polguárd

♛

Who is the Scottish player that is known as a living legend?

   Chessie, the Loch Ness monster.

♛

What do we have to worry about most with development of chess A.I?

It becomes Magnus Carlsentient

♛

Who guards the grandmasters?

Magnus Carlsentry

♛

How do you prove you can spell "grandmaster"?

By putting it into a Magnus Carlsentence

♛

What is a grandmaster's favourite novel?

Magnus CarlSense and Sensibility

How do you consider changing the rules of chess?

    Appealing to the CarlSenate

What do you call a grandmaster who is forgetful?

    Magnus Carlsenile

What does a constipated grandmaster do?

    Use Magnus CarlSenna pods

What grandmaster was the "one and only"?

    Chessney Hawkes

♛

During a chess game, how do you know when the writing's on the wall?

When you re-sign

♛

When should you play for a draw?

When the game begins to *drag* and you have to *pull* yourself through it.

♛

When do you bury a chess game?

When you reach a dead position

♛

How do cows avoid stalemate?

With the fifty moo rule

How do you measure a stalemate?

　The fifty move ruler

How do the Scottish decide a stalemate?

　The Fife-ty move rule

How do the poor decide stalemate?

　The thrifty move rule

Who decides a stalemate?

　The Fifty Move Ruler

♛

How do you describe a player in great confusion?

   Chessed up in the head

♛

What game does Superman always win?

   Faster than a speeding bullet chess

♛

How do slow grandmasters avoid fast play?

   They dodge a bullet chess games

♛

What is a chess player's panacea?

   A magic bullet game

Some people don't believe you can play chess with a minute on the clock until they see the "bulletproof" game.

Many people don't want to play a quick round of chess but sometimes they just have to bite the bullet game.

Playing with just a minute on the clock is extremely nerve racking for me, you could say I was sweating bullets.

It's noble when a classical player takes a bullet game for the good of chess.

When do chess players pay for their membership?

FIDE (Fee Day)

♛

What is the best ELO?

Mr Blue Sky

♛

How is it that a player shows his best moves?

Correspon*dance* chess

♛

What variant does a bad player play?

Correspon*dunce* Chess

♛

Who will tell you the secrets to their chess preparations?

A Candi*date* Master

What do you call a chess player with brain fog?

    A Grandmister

What do you call a chess player who spans across the generations?

    A Grandadmaster

Who gives you permission to play chess?

    A grantmaster

What sort of player makes moves one piece a square at a time?

    A grandularmaster

♛

What type of chess player is employed to work alongside a grandmaster?

    An INTERNational Master

♛

What do you call a chess and player who uses all their efforts energy every move?

    A grandmuster

♛

Grandmaster Jokes

♛

What is Peter Svindler's chess title?

GM: Grünfield Master

♛

What is Simon Williams' chess title?

GM: Ginger Master

♛

What do you call a chess player who tirelessly works their way through lots of games?

A grindmaster

♛

What furniture do all stalemates take place on?

A chess of drawers

♛

What happens with your friend and you keep playing a dead position?

You get a stale-mate

♛

How is playing for a draw like beating a dead horse?

Because you're trying to hit a stalemule

CHESS JOKES

Why is playing the fractions and going for stalemate like treason?

   Because you'll be drawn and quartered

Anyone into parlour games really should keep their cards close to their chess.

How does grandmaster listen to music?

   Play it close to their chess

What happens when a player spills their guts?

   They get it all off their chess

♛

Why should a player avoid eating the crusts of their bread before a match?

   It'll put hairs on their chess

♛

Before doing battle over the board try thumping you chess

♛

What is a grandmasters favourite instruments?

   The Giuoco piano

♛

How do British players begin their chess games?

   With a plain English opening

How do Non-British players begin their games?

   With a broken English opening

How do you describe crazy chess players start a game?

   It's a "For the Bird's" opening

What advice would you give a chess player in prison?

   Play Bird's opening

What should a player do when everything hinges on this game?

   "Fill a doors" defence

♛

What chess variant is recommended when playing in Surrey?

    The Greater London System

♛

What do you call a pig's opening move?

    A Hambit

♛

How does a vampire begin a game of chess?

    With a gambite

♛

What strategy does a grandmaster execute if his breath is smelly?

    Use his chess tic tacs

What is the most important tactic to use when playing the Ancient Greeks?

   Controlling the Centaur

Peter: I'm not playing chess with you if you keep using astrology to make your moves.

   Paul: I was defending my Pisces

How do you cunningly reverse a great disadvantage?

   A zugzwangle

What's the best opportunity for a queen?

   In a pawning window promotion

DANNY TREVANION

Middlegame Jokes

♛

Doctor Doctor! I think I'm becoming a bishop.

Well slide diagonally over here and let me examine you.

♛

Doctor Doctor! I think I'm becoming a chess board.

No, you're just becoming really square.

♛

What is the name for when you're in a confusing match?

   A muddlegame

♛

What is the name for when you playing chess with Harry Potter?

   A mugglegame

♛

Where does a bishop like to live?

   A Fianchatto

♛

When Kasporov lost to a supercomputer he was caught between the devil and the Deep blue...which provided a sea change for the relationship between humans and A.I.

What do you get if cross and English and Scottish player?

   Nigel Shortbread

What tactic does a magician use when playing the black pieces?

   Dynamo counterplay

What are a grandmasters tools to play a game called?

   A war chess

While playing the Giocomo Piano it's important to hit the right key squares.

♛

Why is chess not the most complicated board game?

　Because there is only one place to Go.

♛

What hallmark is the rarest for solid silver English pieces?

　Chesster

♛

What is the uncomfortable state when your opportant attacks two pieces at once with one piece?

　Forkward

♛

When playing a simple computer engine put it in a vulnerable defensive position the CPU will crash with overloading.

What is the danger of studying positional play too march?

   Overworking

In the eye of the pawn storm, be the steady pupil and try not to lash out.

How can an attacker rule the board with a sacrifice?

   Using the law of attraction

What move is favoured most by Dutch players?

   The *Win*dmill

♛

What do you call the fastest pawn structure to get into?

    Sonic (AKA the Hedgehog)

♛

What does Captain Picard fear most when playing chess?

    The Borg defence

♛

What is a farmer's favourite opening?

    The Corn Stalk defence

♛

I saw my opponent playing The Lemming Defence and I couldn't help but follow them...

CHESS JOKES

♛

Imagine my surprise when I learnt the Scotch game isn't having a shot of whiskey after every move.

♛

What is the polite way to apologise for your opening?

"Pardon my French" defence

♛

How do sheriffs like to play chess?

By opening with the Marshall gambit

♛

The Modern day defence is modern day Pirc defence.

♛

What chess playter invented clothes you could iron on yourself?

Prest-on Ware

♛

What is best played on a dusty board?

A polish opening

♛

Is a Spanish player opening with the Neo Catalan declined an insult to the separatist movement?

♛

What do chess players do when they're hungry?

Play the Budapest gambit

♛

What is the scariest move a player can make?

The Halloween gambit

What does a grandmaster play on a bank holiday weekend?

    The Three Knights game

What is the best position if the board is knocked over?

    The Catalan's on it's feet

How does a player play upside down?

    With the Australian gambit

No one ever went broke underestimating the intelligence of the American gambit.

What is the loudest opening?

   The BattanBANG!

Note to self: If your chess board gets flooded it is recommended to use the Wade defence.

15 minutes on the clock – you better start making Rapid strides.

I tried blitzing it at chess and broke my blender.

I 3D printed my chess pieces using jelly and now I'll have a set that didn't set.

I once heard a skeleton attempted chess but he had nobody to play with.

I watched The Seventh Seal in which the main character plays chess with Death. Without knowning their ELO rating I was unsure what the jeopardy was.

What is chess's golden rule?

    The Midas Touch-move rule

What rule feels right to wizards?

    The Magic Touch-move rule

♛

How do you know you can manipulate your pieces?

    The Easy Touch-move rule

♛

How can you stop the resurrection of your opponent's pieces?

    The Healing Touch-move rule

♛

What enforces playing chess in the dark?

    The light touch-move rule

♛

What is enforced when your opponent disappears?

    The lose touch-move rule

What allows the players to move carefully?

   The loose touch-move rule

Imagine my embarrassment when a friend invited me to play OTB and I turned up just in shorts with a bucket and spade.

How do you make pieces out of cheese?

   With a set of chessels

Chess commentator: "Well, that was indeed very unfortunate for Carlsen's play with that piece taken there. It could have happened to a bishop".

♛

What is a Jewish player's favourite time of year?

   Chessvan

♛

How does a gangster lose at chess?

   With a kingpin

♛

Why are silent checkmates special?

   You can hear a pin drop

♛

What do you call a chess automaton without a king and queen on the board?

   A Young Turk

What is the correct term for checkmating with your knight?

    A "pin Sir" movement

Why should you never play in a field?

    Because if you chess with a bull, you get the horns.

What do you call playing chess in ceramic clubs?

    A knight on the tiles

What do you call a chess game that goes lasts into the evening

    Having a late knight

♛

How does a chess player daydream?

   They see castling in the sky

♛

How does a chess player defend underwater?

   By castling pieces adrift

♛

How do chess players remember their best moves?

   They castle their mind back

♛

What is a chess player's favourite music?

   Rook and roll

What is the situation when a hard decision is on the board?

    Between a rook and a hard place

What sport do players play at Christmas?

    Chess boxing day

What do you call writing on a chess piece?

    A chessay

How does a grandmaster relax?

    With Chessential oils

♛

What is a grandmaster's favourite snack?

Chessnuts

♛

What is a chess players favourite instrument?

A Piano-Grandmaster

♛

What's black and white and grey all over?

A chess board

♛

What's black and white and red all over?

A chess board covered in jam

How do you make a grandmaster self-sufficient?

   Give him a Fischer and a chessboard

Give a man a Fischer, Play him for day, Teach a man how to Fischer, play him for a lifetime

What do you uncomfortable chess player during the American VS Russian conflict?

   A Fischer Out of Cold Water

What is a Twitch stream for super grandmasters called?

   A chessuary

What is a grandmasters favourite theme park?

CHESSington World of Adventures

What do you get if you cross a grandmaster and with

ChesSing

They've just launched a dating app for grandmasters called

ChesSingle

What character in *Alice in Wonderland* is a grandmaster?

The Chessure Cat

Endgame Jokes

Which English county are the most grandmasters from?

   Chesshire, followed closely by Chessex

♛

How does a player leave a game in an emergency?

   Using the fire chessacape

♛

What special move is played when a player has a rush of blood to the head?

   En pass out

♛

How do you avoid chess with your uncle?

    Playing en pass aunt

♛

What English move is necessary when a plauer has drunk too much?

    In passing water

♛

What's a grandmasters favourite holiday?

    Chessmas

♛

What do grandmasters do with the latest fancy cheas software

    They are putting on the Fritz

CHESS JOKES

♛

What is it called when your chess software is buggy?

   It's on the Fritz

♛

What site does Pinnocchio use to play?

   Lie chess (Lichess)

♛

What engine is best at 360 chess?

   Stockfischer

♛

What engine is best for Poles?

   Stickfish

♛

What engine do the Teenage Muntant Ninja Turtles never play?

   Shredder

♛

How does a Dragon play chess?

   With the Komodo engine

♛

What chess program guarantees success, no matter the engine you play against?

   Winboard

♛

The engine Rybka translates into English by my unsure grandmaster as "little Fisch-er".

What is a magician's favourite chess engine?

   Houdini

What chess program doesn't hold a candle to all the others?

   Waxman

These chessman look like they're staunt-on winning pieces

What plant is like players with a sore throat?

   A hoarse chess nut

The Queen's Gambit Accepted, is no doubt used by large sways of Netflix viewers.

♛

Who plays like Mark Zukerburg?

Chessy Einseinburg

♛

Where do the most grandmasters in Eastern Europe live?

Chesstonia

♛

How are numbers stored in a chess database?

Chess*base* 10

CHESS JOKES

♛

How do you keep your pass notations moist?

Use Chessbaste

♛

Why was Chessmaster released in versions of thousands, like 3000, 4000, 5000 etc? Is it because their conveying he indeed was a grand-master?

♛

The bearded guy on the front on the Chessmaster games looks like a wizard at math – a mathemagician who can calculate many moves more than you.

♛

What play does a grandmaster make when he's nervous?

A bowel movement

♛

What does a James Bond villian say over a game of chess?

One false move, and you will meet your maker, Mr Bond.

♛

What does is James Bond's signature style of play?
O-O 7

♛

When the game turns when you play your F8

♛

The hardest chess puzzle is one where you haven't begun playing and you're trying to find the missing piece.

♛

What author is best known for using glass beads as pieces?

Hermann Chesse

CHESS JOKES

♛

Thinking too much makes me chessitant to play.

♛

I've created chess puzzles that are impossible to solve. I sculpted hills in my chessboard, after all it's called "the knight's tor".

♛

Chess is imitating life. When paying the other day I didn't remember my PIN and so heard "check, mate".

♛

My last game was like an audit. All checks and balance

♛

My last game in was in VR. I was losing until I gave my opponent a reality check.

♛

I'm very happy with my chess development. In my latest correspondence game I was finally able to exclaim that "the check's in the mail".

♛

When I thought my opponent said gave me a rain check, I thought he had to leave. Turns out water fell onto the pieces and he was one move from mate.

♛

I once played chess with a dyslectic wizard. I lost when he used his spell-check.

♛

I made a chessboard out of springs just so I could finally see a bounced check.

♛

What is a grandmaster's favourite football club?

Manchesster United

♛

What is a wealthy grandmaster's favourite football club?

Manchesster City

♛

What song do Chess player's sing in Church?

I know hymn so well

♛

ABBA weren't very good at puns. This is why the hit song from Chess: The Musical was not called One *Knight* in Bangkok.

♛

How do you tick off a grandmaster in Prague?

Check Republic

♛

How do you finish off a game with your friend in Brno?

Check Mate

♛

What do you call crazy puzzles that changes the rules of chess?

Away with the fairies chess

♛

What compositions are often just wishful thinking?

Airy-Fairy chess

♛

Unbounded boards make for very silly games in my infinite chess wisdom.

Why are squares that are not controlled by pawns like my opening plan of attack?

   They're both full of holes

What stories are full of traps?

   Arabian Knights Mate

How does Batman solve chess puzzles?

   With the Dark Knight's tour

How does a grandmaster prosecute in court?

   They chesstify against the defendant

♛

What do you shout when a when a piece falls off a ship?

    Chessman overboard!

♛

How do chess pieces metamorphorsise?

    They go from rooks to pigs

♛

How should a player experiment in their game?

    Chess tube

♛

What chemical is contained within chessmen?

    Chesstosterone

Where do grandmasters eat?

    A chesstaurant

What do the best chess shops for customers to try out new sets?

    Offer a chess drive

What do you call it when you play with a alien?

    An extra chesstrial

What electric cars do grandmasters drive?

    Chessla

How does a grandmaster play in a forth dimensional hypercube?

    In a chesseract

Why do squares fit together on a board?

    Because they chesselate

What do you call a tetchy player?

    Chessty

How does a player review a match?

    With a chesstimonial

How do you prove a solution for puzzle?

   With a chesstimony

What Nintendo game do grandmasters love to play?

   Chesstris

What are He Man and Skeletor's titles?

   Grandmasters of the Universe

What do you call the best host at a chess banquet?

   Grandmaster of ceremonies

♛

What award is presented to the best chess players who can cook at the same time?

    Grandmasterchef

♛

What do you call an organiser of a Dungeons and Dragon and chess crossover?

    Grandgamemaster

♛

How does Uri Geller win against a grandmaster?

    Bending the rules of chess

♛

What do lazy players use to decide who wins?

    The unwritten rules of chess

What is a confusing match play for grandmasters?

When there are no hard and fast rules of chess

How does a lawyer play?

By using every exception to every rule of chess

How do you play an illegal move?

When you break the laws of chess

How does a player give attention to detail to the rules?

They follow the letter of the laws of chess

Why is a player perpetually unlucky?

    Because it's Murphy's laws of chess

♛

How is does a player become most wanted?

    Be on the wrong side of the laws of chess

♛

Why does the player with the most pieces usually win?

    Because possession is nine parts of the laws of chess

♛

Remember to keep your pieces in a tool chess, so you always have the right one a for the job. After all, only a bad chessman would blame his tools.

CHESS JOKES

What is a grandmaster's favourite comfort food?

    Macaroni Chess

How do you make the king and queen laugh?

    Send in the Royal chesster

Where do players like to stay when they go to Vegas?

    The MGM Grandmaster

What grandmaster did Dick Whittington play on the way to London?

    Chess in Boots

♛

Why does Postman Pat have a black and white cat?

So he can have a game Chess early in the morning, when the day is dawning.

♛

How do Catholic grandmasters address their priests?

"Chess me father, for I have sinned"

♛

Are you sure you can play on a checkers board?

Well chess and no

♛

How do you agree with a knight's position?

"Chess Sir"

What is considered an old grandmaster?

   When they're over knighty years of age

Why is is it rude to interrupt a grandmaster in the evening?

   Because they only have their knighties on

What do you call a chess referee who doesn't care about the rules?

   An arbitrary arbiter

In my last game I was totally crushing my opponent. I lost badly, but I really fancied him.

♛

How can you gage the atmosphere of a great tournament?

By breathing in the sweet smell of suc-chess

♛

Who is a grandmaster's favourite chef?

Cheston Blumenthal

♛

How is a copper mineral like a novice player?

They're both chessylite

♛

What grandmaster is the best strategist?

TacticIan Nepomniachtchi

What is Jay-Z's opinion about chess software?

"I've got knighty nine problems but a Fritz ain't one"

What's the first sign a grandmaster might have the flu?

They have a chessty cough

CHECKMATE!

You won the game.

Thank you for getting to the end of this book. Please leave a positive review if any of these jokes made you laugh. And if they were all terrible, leave a positive review anyway and play a joke on someone else!
- All the best, Danny

Contact me if you have little else to do: dannytrevanionjokes@gmail.com

And on social media:
@dannytrevanion

NOTES

Printed in Great Britain
by Amazon